Secret
Jews
In Portugal

Lionel Yasef

SECRET JEW - Crypto Jews = Jews who practiced or practice Judaism in secret, they never stopped practicing the Jewish faith but with specific characteristics and different from orthodox Judaism.

In Portugal they lived many Jews in almost all the territory for so many centuries I ask the historians and archaeologists gentlemen, because only appear in our days remains of two or three synagogues? Continue to be references there in the streets, bars, neighborhoods the "Jewish quarters "but synagogues symbols or other memories, not only even some people who hide and could witness this past," Marranism "but this seems to be contradictory also to the Jews of Slavonic origin or German-speaking, appears here a certain indifference that smothers the story . Will Catholics took the time to destroy as many heritage hide traces, was the Holocaust architectural heritage in relation to Judaism? It seems so, this method also the Arabs are using, it seems that Catholics and Arabs share many ideas.

The "Portuguese Marranos" are living monuments of the history of Judaism.

iberia = Jewish land   Sefarad = Spain / Iberia / West

SECRET JEW - Crypto Jews = Jews who practiced or practice Judaism in secret, they never stopped practicing the Jewish faith but with specific characteristics and different from orthodox Judaism.

BNEI ANUSIM - descendants of New Christians are not considered new because were born Christians, this term can be misleading.

MARRANO - new Christian - recently converted to Christianity. many confuse with secret Jew.

In Portugal, we have cities without Jews without "Judaism", but with "Jewish quarters"

means were just buildings and streets. The "Holy" Inquisition was effective? He cleared the cities of the Jewish presence or something else? Did the Jews in Portugal were even secret because of the violence of persecution? was what then happened to "Judaism"? Only here and there were some architectural, culinary notes, some sentences files, and little else? We will propose to the Portuguese knowledge of their roots and the Jewish Resurgence,

.

The Captives (benei anussin)

The Romans surrounded the city and the temple of Jerusalem: (Obadiah 20)

"And the captives of this host of the children of Israel shall possess the Canaanites to Zarephath; and the captivity of Jerusalem, which is in Sepharad".

The yahudim of yahrushalayim (Jerusalem) where did? In Sepharad, meaning "Spain or Ispania".

Jews who escaped from Roman captivity, crossed Africa, Ethiopia, and crossed the Strait of Iberian and came to Iberia (the original term "heberia", which means Land of Hebrews), which was in the south of Ispania (Spain = Sepharad).

In the year 1492, the Catholic kings of Spain gave an ultimatum to the Sephardic Jews, or became Christians or had to leave Spain; good they chose to leave Spain, and went to Portugal, also had to leave Portugal by order of King Manuel and went to territories in Europe, the Netherlands, England and the Ottoman Empire, Istanbul and Thessaloniki, later with the Dutch and Portuguese came to the Americas. So many escape Inquisitive sword of Christianity being the most in the US, having been some scattered Portugal and Brazil.

For those who suffer and have suffered persecution, they are by discriminated political reasons and taken to religious courts, which is a bad idea when it comes to Portuguese Jews who for centuries were persecuted in sentences of religious courts to the point that even in our days be hard to face religious courts even rabbinic where are "respondents" and their intimacy called into question and their faith and their struggle, and after all this attitude is (anti-Semitic), the Portuguese "Portuguese Marranos" are living monuments of history of Judaism.

Reconstruction of identities

"I believe what I believe"

The Marranism in Brazil

The Portuguese Marranos were linked to their own identity by conscience or by self-knowledge, assigning value to the image they had of themselves. The concern with this image led them to disobey, to rebel, but also led them to obey even more, if only in the public domain. Thus, in the intimacy of the house took on Jewish identity and before the general society sought only social identity that enabled them to be included in the colonial situation.

The nature of the revolt against the aggressions of catholic clerical power to the Marrano's self-image is different from a revolt against economic or simply political mechanisms. It is the self-image caused individual. The idea of social dignity is well known in the strategies of the Marranos when seeking to safeguard their own religious affiliation through cultural syncretism. In defense of this social dignity it was included duty, by each of these individuals to maintain Judaism practices, even clandestinely.

The descendants of "New Christians " was imposed a number of social taboos.

Forbiden entry into the profession of arms or in public office, among other limitations . The concept of blood purity was used in the sixteenth century, to distinguish that racial and politically, fell within the ideal Portuguese white and "Old Christians".

It is interesting to note that, historically, the terms - old Christian and new Christian - portray significantly contradictory aspects and radical consequences. In the early years of preaching Christianity, the dissidence created the category of old Christians as referring to Christians of Jewish origin and new Christians, the gentile origin were appointed.

It also seems interesting to study, how, in the historical memory of the Northeastern population in Brazil was rooted a set of real and imagined events memories that lasted until the times

We shall not stop the historical facts that marked out the way Portugal and Spain claimed political authority over the new lands that would be known as Brazil. Interesting study, to what extent there is relationship between the medieval imagination, brought by the Portuguese to Brazil, and the Iberian Jewish culture (Sefarad).

The attitudes of Sephardic were shaped by life experience in the Iberian Peninsula. And in each country where they walked, they redefined the concepts of their identities in the relations that should establish whether the Gentiles or other groups of Jews that perhaps existed in those places.

They found in the "mental reservation" how to circumvent the inquisitorial vigilance and neighbors to keep active, at least, what was tradition in Judaism. This pattern of resistance consisted of mental replacement devices of Christian figures by another Jewish. So reports Lipiner (1999: 214):

New Christians watched the new worship in churches, muttering to each other sentences and restrictive expressions. Should pronounce mentally such formulas without that words with his lips . In Brazil, during the Holy

Office Visitation in Pernambuco, the visitor, on December , 1594, filed a complaint against the New Christian surgeon Ferdinand Soeiro that "the Mass, when the priest, raising the sacred host was seen to be on his knees and beating their breasts to hide, but pronouncing :**"I believe what I believe"** .

Should be interested in the study of the continuities of an Iberian Jewish culture in the context of colonial Brazilian Jewish community, the acculturation conditions the "Marranos" population transferred from Portugal to Brazil, the symbolic representations of the North eastern mixed population and its transformations.

Portuguese Marranos

Rare example of medieval Jewish temples

and Portuguese pre-Renaissance art, the Synagogue of Tomar

is the only, this time, fully conserved still existing

in Portugal. It was built in the mid-fifteenth century

purposely to religious function, which shows the

financial availability of the Jewish community here

resident, its strength and its prosper.

In addition to the function for which it was built, also

served as a school, assembly and Tomar Jewish community court.

It was closed in 1496, when the King Manuel edict of expulsion of the Jews, after which it was converted into a prison; in the seventeenth century is such as the Hermitage of St. Bartholomew; in the nineteenth century it was hayloft,barn, warehouse grocery stores, wine cellar and storage.

There is nowhere in the world except in Jerusalem, being a living example that came to our days due to very strong Jewish presence in this region we call "Espania" that in biblical terms means West .

Interestingly the story of Portuguese is over the well-connected centuries, Sefarad would be a very strong presence at the origin of what is now Portugal, unlike other regions, "Ashkenazi" as Russia, Poland etc which does not have a unique historical monument not be recent.

There are two orifices in each of the upper corners where the mouths of clay jars can be found, fitted face downwards inside the walls, which were used to enhance the temple acoustics.

One is partially visible to make its purpose clearer.

In 1923, Samuel Schwarz, a Jewish mining engineer from Poland who had come to Portugal six years earlier, bought the Synagogue and restored it from the state of neglect into which it had fallen. He donated it to the Portuguese state (in 1939) to house the Museu Luso-Hebraico de Abraão Zacuto.

(Abraham Zacuto Luso- Jewish Museum).

Tomar-Portugal

The Museum collection consists of tombstones from various areas of Portugal. Excavation work in the annexe uncovered coins from the reign of King Afonso V (1448-1481) –confirming the probable date of the construction of the Synagogue – ceramics for domestic use and the system used to heat the water for the Mikvah, or ritual purification bath. There are also other items associated with Jewish culture, religious items, remembrances from visitors and a documentary collection.

Portuguese Jews were after D.Manuel almost all, or at least those who had money to Constantinople in Turkey, Thessaloniki in Greece that is within the Ottoman Empire where they were protected in the case of Greece until they leave the Turks had no problems,

others went to Amsterdam where they founded the first synagogue of the region and from Amsterdam went to Brazil with the Dutch, interestingly were also with the Dutch to North America where the first synagogue was also founded as happened in Brazil. We can say that the Portuguese Jews were the pioneers of the Jewish Diaspora in the New World and the Old North Europe and because Askenasi ude Sefarad origin with other influences such later Germanophilism or Slavonic countries. Called Sephardic - derived from Sefarad, the Hebrew name of Iberia - Iberian Jews still settled in the Roman Empire time, knowing a period of great economic and social growth during the great period muçulmano.uma of these Jews took refuge in land near the border with Spain.

Once they had been forced to baptism and remained Jews, these men and women formed closed communities who practiced the Jewish worship in secret and had no contact with the outside. thus were born the crypto-Jews portugueses.foi decisive Jews intervention beside D. Afonso Henriques, in making Lisbon in 1147) and granting them privileges for the assistance provided in the settlement of the territory. Communities widened up, so that the reign of King Dinis (1278-1324) had Jewish communes scattered across the country.

At the end of the fifteenth century would live in Portugal around 30 000 Jews.

MY GRANDPARENTS WERE THESE TRADITIONS THAT REMEMBER

SOMETIMES

THOUGHT THAT WERE STRANGE BUT NOBODY WAS TALKING.

Nogueira, Monteiro Borralho

Portuguese Secret Jwe

I used to kiss any piece of bread that falls to the ground.

The blood fell to the ground in the animal slaughter was covered with earth.

Eggs with blood stain were thrown away.

Avoid working on Saturdays. Saturday was the day of the bath well taken and wear new clothes.

Taught to the children the legend that point star was growing warts on fingers.

Tradition of not throwing food out and enjoy everything.

In general they were religious, with faith but without saints and images.

Use of terms such as "massada" (a Jewish fortress that was destroyed), or "pay siza "state taxes"(Siza is imposed in Hebrew) or " mezuras" (reverence to the mezuzah). Even expressions like "the "carapuça" in Ladino ,shoe served," which is a reference to hats used by Jews in the Middle Ages to differentiate from non-Jews.

Portuguese pita "bolo de caco" from Madeira Island

Tradition of Portuguese Jwes

Funeral rites

Cover all the mirrors in the house.

Cut the nails of the deceased.

Wash the body of a dead man. dressing the body in white clothes, the shrouds, "mortalha".

The body was hidden for a day, and then a procession led him to the cemetery.

Throw a handful of earth on the coffin when it was lowered into the grave.

Almost no one entered or left during this period.

Men do not shave for thirty days.

Keep the place of the deceased at the table , do not eat meat for a week after a death in the family.

Swearing by the rest of a dear dead or the soul of the mother or father.

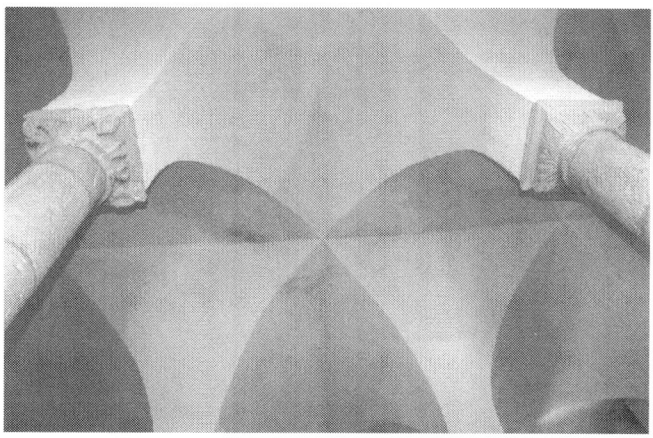

The Synagogue of Tomar , *best preserved of the medieval synagogues of Portugal*

Because those emotions ,(little things)that you do not know well?

It is in your heart and anytime awakens in you this Restlessness this whirlwind of emotions that unknown nostalgia, feel the blessing and nothing else matters because it was God that opened you the sacred door of being.

It is the burning bush at Sinai, something that burns inside you without stopping, can be a Utopia or will the memory be to speak up?

People is chosen by God, the People of God chooses God.

For whatever reason you were chosen .

You will be accepted, do not be afraid and accept what God offers you, this is very important in your life, may not make sense, but you must accept the blessing of God.

Rab. Isaac Aboab da Fonseca (1605-1693) Born in Castro D´aire Portugal

Sephardi rabbi. Aboab was born in Castro Daire, Portugal, of a Marrano family. At the age of 21, Aboab was appointed *ḥakham* of the congregation Bet Israel. In 1641, following the Dutch conquests in *Brazil, Aboab joined the Amsterdam Jews who established a community at (Pernambuco) as their *ḥakham*, thus becoming **the first American rabbi**. Morteira having recently died, Aboab was appointed *ḥakham* as well as teacher in the *talmud torah*, principal of the yeshivah, and member of the *bet din*; in this capacity he was one of the signatories of the ban of excommunication issued against Spinoza also Portuguese marrano,1656. Aboab became celebrated as a preacher, and some of his sermons and eulogies have been published. It was a pulpit address delivered by Aboab in 1671 which prompted the construction of the magnificent synagogue of the Sephardi community in Amsterdam; he preached the first sermon in the new building on its dedication four years later. fession of Sins," Amsterdam, 1666). His most ambitious production was a rendering of the Pentateuch in Spanish together with a commentary (*Parafrasis Commentada sobre el Pentateucho*, Amsterdam, 1688).

synagogue of the Portuguese Sephardi community in Amsterdam

Near the entrance to the synagogue is a memorial wall filled with the names of B'nai Anusim who were tried and punished by the Inquisition for secretly practicing Judaism, including some who were publicly burned at the stake in the 18th century, nearly three centuries after their ancestors had been dragged to the baptismal font.

Guarda district in Portugal's northeastern interior, the charming village of Trancoso was home to a flourishing Jewish community prior to the expulsion and forced conversion of Portugal's Jews in 1497.

On typical Jewish homes, for example, the windows were laid out in a decidedly asymmetrical fashion, at varying heights and lengths, creating a sense of architectural imperfection and inadequacy.

of the medieval homes have crosses engraved adjacent to the entrance as an ostensible statement of piety. Fearful of running afoul of the watchful eyes of the Inquisition, Trancoso's B'nai Anusim also engaged in this practice, albeit with a twist.

The bottom of the etching, they added what appear to be three prongs, as if holding up the cross. But to Jewish eyes, it is clear what their real intention was, as the three spokes clearly form an inverted "Shin," the Hebrew letter that is often used to denote one of the Divine names.

This was how Trancoso's hidden Jews sought to cling to their heritage, subtly indicating that they had not forgotten, nor abandoned, the faith of their forefathers.

It is in memory of their tenacity that we gathered dozens of their descendants, all of them Portuguese B'nai Anusim, to take part in the ceremony this past Sunday. Symbolically, we began the procession with the Torah facing a large and imposing cathedral in the very same public square where the Inquisition had once tormented Trancoso's hidden Jews.

Portuguese B'nai Anusim

Speaking to the assembled crowd, my voice cracked with emotion as I pointed at the basilica and told the B'nai Anusim, "we are here today because your forefathers did not surrender to those who sought to force them to abandon their faith. They bravely and stubbornly clung to their Jewishness in secret, risking everything.

I feel that the "barbed wire " continues to separate the Jews .

 Portuguese origin and "secret Jew", but for Israel can only be a tourist.

Israel has forty thousand illegal without resolution, this strange campaign against the "Marranos of Portugal", alienating the Jews descendants such as my daughters feel not Welcome among the Israelites in Israel, strange thing, retained in the "Egypt"again.

The first titles of nationality granted by Portugal to Thessaloniki Israelites were awarded by the Portuguese Government on the initiative of the Chargé d'Affaires and Consul in Constantinople, in 1912/1913, convinced Lisbon to grant them with the explicit aim to consolidate the external prestige of the Republic, establishing a Portuguese influence in the Levant, expanding export trade and gaining market share for Portuguese products.

The Consul mentions the registration of 384 families of Thessaloniki; other times speaks in 500. Among the objections of the Greeks to accept "nationalitie" acquired after his entry into the city and the fire that devastated in 1917 and did not leave papers, do not know. The oldest list found contains 580 names of people, arranged by families and although undated, the correspondence leads to the inference that has been made between 1926 and 1927. Although some names (55) are noted as "devenu Hellenic" it is possible that this list no longer includes people who left the great wave of emigration of 1915/1916 - and it is certain that people appear registered in Paris as" born in Thessaloniki "whose name was not on the aforementioned list.

Note that, in the Ottoman Empire, Portugal, like other Christian , benefited from the capitulations regime, also called "protection" and that translated into roles of European nationalities that were only valid on the Turkish for purposes good society and tax evasion. Between 1843 and 1912 there were cases of attribution of Portuguese nationality the Ottoman Jews, perhaps insignificant in numbers, but the relevant precedent: Cairo, Alexandria, Adrianople, Athens, Smyrna, Constantinople.A point of comparison: not mistaken, in 1916, the heads of families enrolled in the Jewish Community of Lisbon counted 180, a number that will be maintained in the 20s.

Touro synagogue

"The Touro Synagogue is not only the oldest synagogue in America, but also one of its most ancient symbols of freedom. There is no better tradition than the story of the contributions of the Touro Synagogue to the objectives of freedom and justice for all. "

John F. Kennedy, President of the United States,

September 15, 1963

Touro synagogue

Portuguese-American Jewish

Bearing the name of a Portuguese-American Jewish family with roots in Tomar, Touro Synagogue, Newport, Rhode Island, it was devoted to December 7, 1763, on the first day of Hanukkah, and remains today the oldest synagogue in the United States - the only of the colonial period that still survives and remains in business. The congregation was founded in 1658 (only 4 years after the arrival of the first Portuguese Jews to New York) by Sephardic Jews, mostly Marranos and the descendants of Marranos who had initially fled the Portuguese Inquisition and escaping now persecutions in the Caribbean to the Spaniards. Among the community's founders were counted Mordecai Campanal Moses Israel

Pacheco, Simão Mendes and Abraham Burgos. The religious leader was called Isaac Touro - and one of his sons, Judah Touro would be down in history as one of the largest American benefactors of the nineteenth century. But about him I promise to write another day.

Initially unable to build its own synagogue, the community of Portuguese Jews of Newport gathered in private homes on the nights of Friday and on Saturday mornings.

During its first century of stay in Rhode Island (the first colony of the 13 original American colonies to declare independence from Great Britain), the Portuguese Jews prospered, becoming artisans and merchants respected in overwhelmingly Protestant colony. Their success attracted a migratory influx of Sephardic Jews and Ashkenazi (Eastern European Jews with roots in the Hebrew word Ashkenaz, meaning Germany), who joined the initial community, taking together the traditional religious rituals of the Jews of Spain and Portugal . With the community's growth came the need to find a permanent place for holding religious services, and it turned to other communities of Portuguese Jews. The first answer came from Shearith Israel congregation, New York, the oldest in the country, who sent a generous contribution of £ 149,060. Other congregations of Portuguese Jews - including Jamaica, Curacao, Suriname and London - also provided financial assistance for the construction of the synagogue.

Peter Harrison, the most famous American architect of the eighteenth century, offered to do the building project, which took four years to build, is dedicated to December 2, 1763 by the congregation rabbi, the Luso-American Isaac Touro.

The dedication ceremony for the building was attended by many notable among the Protestant elite Newport. The Touro Synagogue is considered one of the most emblematic works of Peter Harrison, among which include the Kings Chapel, Boston, and the Church of Christ in Cambridge, both in the state of Massachusetts.

The Portuguese Synagogue in Newport

With the synagogue and a cemetery acquired years before the Portuguese congregation could now meet three of the essential functions of Jewish communal life - the actual religious rituals, education of children and funerals. The congregation of Portuguese Jews of Newport chose for himself the name of Yeshuat Israel (Salvation).

During the American Revolutionary War, and because of

the British blockade of the port city, much of the community escaped to New York. After the conflict, the vitality of the congregation rekindled itself. The fact that during the war many of the public buildings in the city have been damaged, the Touro Synagogue was also used for general meetings of Rhode Island and the state Supreme Court.

In 1790, at the invitation of Rabbi Moses Seixas, President George Washington visit this Synagogue of Portuguese Jews and days after sending them a letter that would be for history, reaffirming the principles of equality and religious tolerance that guided the American Constitution: "(...) Because fortunately, the US government, which does not give sanction to intolerance or persecution assistance (...) ". These words were written a year before the Bill of Rights, which still applied only to the federal government.

Alongside the Synagogue Touro, the cemetery of the Sephardim congregation of Newport is another testimony to the size and weight of the Newport community.

"Shearith Israel's goal has been and remains to ensure that the Touro Synagogue, including the precious rimonim, remains intact, available for the continued use of Jews as an active place of worship and the continuous benefit of all people of faith as well as all those touched by its rich and inspiring history," the statement said.

A lawyer for the Newport congregation, Gary Naftalis, said the judge was "completely correct on the facts and the law."

"There's no merit to any appeal here," Naftalis said.

In 1790, George Washington sent a letter to the Touro congregation pledging America's commitment to religious liberty.

Synagogue Touro, of Newport

Most Portuguese Jews from Portugal, and then from Amsterdam, where some sailed with Dutch merchants to **South America,** settling in the city of **Recife**.

There they built the **first synagogue in the Americas,** Kahal Zur Israel Synagogue.(Brazil)

Twenty-three sailed to Port Royal, Jamaica,then, on the French ship Sainte Catherine, they arrived in 1654 at the **Dutch Colony of New Amsterdam,** becoming the **first Jews in North America**.

Dutch Governor Peter Stuyvesant attempted to expel them, but they were allowed to stay, as the Dutch West India Company in Holland considered Spain and Portugal its main enemies, not Jews or other dissenters.

 In 1730, **Jewish citizens in New York**bought land and built the small **"Mill Street Synagogue,"** the **first Jewish house of worship in North America**.

During the colonial era, America's population grew to 3 million, with a **Jewish population of around 2,000 in seven Sephardic congregations:**

Shearith Israel, **New York City**, begun 1655;
Yeshuat Israel, **Newport, Rhode Island**, begun 1658;
Mickve Israel, **Savannah, Georgia**, begun 1733;
Mikveh Israel, **Philadelphia**, begun 1740;
Shaarai Shomayim, **Lancaster, Pennsylvania**, begun 1747;
Kahal Kadosh Beth Elohim, **Charleston, South Carolina**, begun 1749; and Kahal Kadosh Beth Shalom, **Richmond, Virginia**, begun 1789.

From the 3rd century on, the teaching of **Rabbi Samuel in Babylonia**, that **'the law of the land is the law'**, resulted in Jews refraining from trying to change their political situation.

At the end of the fifteenth century there were more than 140 Jewish quarters, distributed by the main towns of Portugal , including the Azores and Madeira,

WHERE ARE THE RESPECTIVE (AT LEAST) 140 SYNAGOGUES IN PORTUGAL ?! **Confiscated and transformed into Catholic churches.**

CASA DO CASTELO -SABUGAL

Secret cabinets inside the walls

"Hechal" is for Sephardic Jews the term for the cupboard or the recess of a wall towards Israel, where they keep the Torah scrolls (Sifrei Torah).

The name comes from the Hebrew (לְ כִי.ה palace, expression used in different times of the Temple of Jerusalem, to refer to the sanctuary where was the Holy of Holies.

By Lyonel Yafe

Portuguese Secret Jews

ISBN-13: 978-1539512349

ISBN-10: 1539512347

Made in the USA
Monee, IL
07 March 2024

54592154R10033